ROLLER SK
AND RACK~ ~ ~

Devonshire Park and tennis
in Eastbourne

The First 125 Years

S. B. Publications

First published in 1999 by S. B. Publications,
c/o 19 Grove Road, Seaford, East Sussex BN25 1TP

ISBN 1 85770 156 9

Designed, edited and typeset by CGB, Lewes
Printed by Adland Print Group Ltd
Unit 10-11, Franthorne Way, Bellingham Trading Estate, London SE6 3BX.
Tel: 0181 695-6262

CONTENTS

ACKNOWLEDGEMENTS

Many people have contributed greatly to the production of this book. A special thank you to Amanda Wilkins for research and interviews; Richard Crook for permission to use information from his *Life of Henry Currey;* Bill Leach of Chatsworth Estates; Beverley Ebdy of Eastbourne Theatres, John Haylett, copy editor of *Ace,* magazine of the Lawn Tennis Association; also the staff of Eastbourne Reference Library, East Sussex County Council's Records Offices at Lewes, and for photographs and illustrations the Eastbourne Civic Society, Allsport, Adland Print Group, Corel WTA Tour and A and L Photography.

FOREWORD

On July 1, 125 years ago, Devonshire Park opened its gates to the public. Like so much in Eastbourne it owes its beginning and much of its later development to William Cavendish, 7th Duke of Devonshire. It was his architect, Henry Currey, who designed the Winter Garden; it was his orchestra which gave regular concerts in the Pavilion; and it was he who five years later, approved the setting out of courts for the new game of lawn tennis.

Music and tennis were the principal attractions in the eleven acre park when it was administered by the Devonshire Park and Baths Company. In 1946 Eastbourne Corporation took over and had to decide how best to use the assets it had acquired for the good of the town and ultimate benefit of its ratepayers.

Wisely, as it turned out, it chose to concentrate on tennis. Someone must have had a crystal ball for all sport was in the doldrums in the immediate post war years. How could anyone foresee that it was to become one of the most popular spectator sports, that its star performers would earn fortunes and that, from 1975, the eyes of the world would be on Eastbourne in the week before Wimbledon?

Here is the full story, and pictures, of the first 125 years of Devonshire Park – Eastbourne's International Lawn Tennis Centre.

Councillor Beryl Healy
Mayor of Eastbourne
Spring 1999

1

THE BUILDING BEGINS

Today, in the world of international tennis, Eastbourne's Devonshire Park is acknowledged to be one of three top venues for tournaments on grass – Wimbledon and Queen's Club are the others. Since 1975 the International Ladies Lawn Tennis Championships have been played there in the week prior to the Wimbledon Fortnight and its season also includes the South of England Veterans' Championships and the Inter County Cup Grass Court Championships.

Wimbledon started with croquet. It was not until 1875 that a tennis court was marked out on one of its lawns. Devonshire Park started with cricket in 1875 and roller skating a year later. The first game of tennis was played there in April 1880.

The man with the vision, the land and the money to do for Eastbourne what he had done for Buxton was William Cavendish, 7th Duke of Devonshire. And it was thanks largely to him and his architect, Henry Currey, that Eastbourne with its wide tree-lined boulevards and houses of classic design became known as 'Eastbourne the Elegant, the Empress of Watering Places', a resort built by gentlemen for gentlemen.

The first phase of the development of Eastbourne by the Duke and another bright young businessman, John Davies Gilbert, began shortly after the arrival of the railway. They owned most of the land between the Downs and the sea and were quick to appreciate that once a rail link was established it would be more profitable to develop their rolling acres rather than farm them.

It was during the second phase of the development of the Duke's estates that it was decided to build houses on Eastbourne Cricket Club's

The Devonshire Park Swimming baths and, below, the raised terraces and flower borders of the South Walk.

ground behind Terminus Road and on the marshland adjoining it and provide an alternative pitch elsewhere. The Duke's intention 'to appropiate for the purpose of cricket and a recreation ground a plot of land, eleven and one half acres in extent, situated to the west of the town and and near the Eastbourne College,' was revealed to the readers of the *Eastbourne Chronicle* on November 22, 1873. It seemed it was no sooner read than done.

The 'plot of land' named on the plans as Devonshire Park, was planted with a variety of trees and shrubs and landscaped to provide raised terraces and tree lined walks around a new cricket ground laid with turf from the club's old pitch.

It opened to the public on July 1 1874 and a week later the first cricket match to be played there was between the newly formed Devonshire Park Cricket Club and an Eastbourne College XI. The result, for the record, was a draw in favour of the host side as there was not time for its players to complete a second innings.

Next to the new park was the lofty Italianate style tower with which George Wallis, the designer of the new swimming baths, had disguised the chimney of the heating system which

The baths chimney tower dominated the Carlisle Road skyline for nearly a century.

kept the water at a constant 68° degrees Fahrenheit.

The gentlemen's swimming bath was 166ft long; the ladies 122ft; and both were filled direct from the open sea through filters at high tide. The sea water came in through a large pipe laid beneath Carlisle Road from the beach near the Wish Tower. Not all of it was intended for use in the baths, which opened in April 1874. It was also sold by the three gallon bucketful at threepence for hot water, twopence for cold, to anyone wishing to buy their own bathful. It would be 'delivered daily to all parts of the town by the Company's Vans,' states a prospectus of the 1890s – the company being the Devonshire Park and Baths Company of which the Duke was the major shareholder.

The next project in the park was the outdoor skating rink. A crowd of some 300, fewer than expected because of the rain which did not stop until 4pm, attended the opening at 4.30pm on July 1 1875 and saw a display by the president of the New York Roller Skating Association and the inventor of the roller skate, J L Plimpton, and his two daughters. The *Eastbourne Gazette* described the occasion:

> 'Considerable interest was created in the proceedings. Mr Plimpton and his two daughters displayed remarkable ability in the performances on the rink. In fact, the Misses Plimpton achieved wonderful ornamental movements with the skates. . .

Behind the rink the Winter Garden was being built. The first part, the Floral Hall, was completed by August 1875 and provided a combined indoor and outdoor skating area for up to 500 skaters. They could swoop around indoors to the music of Herr Wolff's band, which was brought along

The Floral Hall.

from the pier for the skating sessions and, when the glass doors were thrown open in fine weather, glide onto the rink outside.

The Floral Hall, as its name implies, was an exceedingly large conservatory. Vines wound their way up the cast iron columns; creepers trailed down from the glass roof; beds of flowers and shrubs bordered the floor. It was used as a concert hall, the Eastbourne Horticultural Society's Chrysanthemum Show was held there each November, and it was much in demand for banquets, meetings, exhibitions and bazaars.

The rest of the Winter Garden 'from the plans of Mr Henry Currey Architect to His Grace the Duke of Devonshire' was completed a year later. The *Eastbourne Gazette* had had sight of the plans. The building, it told its readers on November 4 1875, measured 150ft by 150ft and the height to the top of the central vane was 85ft.

> 'It contains a large winter garden (the Floral Hall) and skating rink . . . a refreshment saloon, four billiards rooms and a concert room 88ft by 44ft . . . A large proportion of the roof is glazed and the remainder is of zinc . . . One side

The Winter Garden Pavilion viewed from the north east and, below, the Pavilion set out for a concert.

of the building faces the cricket field and here are the usual pavilion, dressing rooms and other offices and elsewhere are two commodious reading rooms, near the main entrance by variation of the ground, about nine feet above the general floor level. . .'

The concert room, or Pavilion as it came to be called, had a fine oak parquet floor and was also used for social reunions and for balls. The first Grand Concert staged there was on July 5, 1876. Ticket prices ranged from 10s 6d (52½p) for a seat in the stalls to four shillings (20p) unreserved and the list of artists was headed by the 'Welsh Nightingale', Madame Edith Wynne. However she telegraphed at the last minute to say her physician considered she was 'too unwell to make the journey to Eastbourne' and the English operatic soprano, Madame Blanche Cole, deputised for her. In spite of the defection of its principal singer the concert was a great success and almost immediately a permanent orchestra was formed to give regular concerts in the Pavilion.

Ten years later there was trouble. Julian Adams, the conductor who was responsible in those days for Eastbourne's reputation for good music, was replaced by Albert Kettemus from the Hallé Orchestra. The cause of the split was a quarrel between Adams and his employers, the Devonshire Park and Baths Company. It was conducted by both sides in full public view through the correspondence columns of Eastbourne's two newspapers.

A short article in the *Eastbourne Chronicle*, published together with a letter from Adams 'conceived in a most hostile spirit to the Park directors and their management' brought an immediate response from the chairman, Robert Insoll. He claimed that Adams had at first denied writing the letter, but when it was shown to be in his handwriting he admitted writing it but said he had decided not to send it. It had reached the paper as a result of a misunderstanding with a friend to whom he had shown it. The departing conductor put his case in a long letter to the *Eastbourne Gazette*. He complained that his position was made untenable by the manager of the Devonshire Park Theatre, A Standen Triggs, usurping his power as director of concerts.

By the end of the 1880s everything had settled down. The orchestra had fifty instrumentalists and was conducted in the summer season, when it was called the Devonshire Park Grand Orchestra, by Norfolk Megone. In the winter it was known as the Duke of Devonshire's Orchestra and conducted by Pierre Tass.

The man behind this musical initiative, and the initial provider of the fetes and firework displays, the circuses and skating carnivals and other lavish entertainments in the park was Captain Thomas Holman, secretary to the Devonshire Park and Baths Company. He had, presumably, to balance the books, as can be seen from the scale of charges set out in the company's prospectus of 1879 – the year Eastbourne Corporation made the first of a number of unsuccessful attempts to purchase the park.

Admission......Sixpence
Bathchairs.......One shilling
A charge of sixpence is made for the use of Plimpton Skates

	A Year	6 months	1 month	Fortnight
Subscription Ticket	40s	30s	15s	10s

There were discounts for family tickets but holders of them were warned that they were liable to forfeited if used by other than a family member or a friend staying at the family home. Visitors had more to pay if they wished to skate on the one and a half acres of indoor and outdoor rinks which were open between 11am and 1pm; 4pm and 6pm and from 7.30 to 9.30pm. A year's skating subscription was one guinea, reducing from fifteen shillings for six months down to four shillings for a fortnight.

Anyone wishing to play cricket, croquet, bowls, lawn tennis, badminton or try his or her hand at archery had to join the clubs running these sports. The fee for each club for the season was five shillings, and potential members had to provide satisfactory references. The Board of Management also reserved to itself the right to name certain days, should it see fit to do so, when tickets would not be available.

'Any information required, or complaints to be made, address THOMAS HOLMAN, Secretary' appears at the bottom of the handbill.

By imposing charges that could be afforded only by the reasonably well-to-do the Devonshire Park and Baths Company maintained the select tone of the park and its facilities. By doing so it did not endear itself to the majority of the town's working population and many changes were to be made and many years to pass before Devonshire Park was as popular with the people of Eastbourne as it was with the resort's high season visitors.

Meanwhile construction work was still going on. It seemed that after every winter there would be a new building or attractions the following spring. A concert in the Floral Hall on July 18 1881 began in gas light and ended bathed in electric light: 'giving it the appearance of a miniature Crystal Palace. . . or one of the enchanted palaces to be read of in *The Arabian Nights,*' wrote an obviously impressed *Eastbourne Chronicle* reporter. The *Illustrated London News* was equally complimentary:

'There is not a finer pleasure ground anywhere, belonging to a town of this class, than Devonshire Park, named after the Duke, who is the chief proprietor of Eastbourne. The whole of these grounds, as well as the Floral Hall, is now illuminated at nights by Messrs Siemens' system of electric lighting, the apparatus being worked by two 10 horse power engines, at the base of the swimming baths.'

The Duke went along to look at the lights and wrote in his diary:

'They are quite brilliant.'

Three years later two more buildings opened – a racquets court, 'erected at great expense'; and the Henry Currey-designed Devonshire Park Theatre.

The two Swiss chalets on the College Road side of the park, one with dressing rooms and a central booking hall for the tennis courts, the other an afternoon tea house, were proving popular with visitors as were the exhibitions of 'plain and ornamental swimming' given regularly in the Devonshire Baths by the Champion Lady Swimmer of All England, Miss Laura Saigeman.

Sycamore Grove

The afternoon concerts among the exotic trees and shrubs of the Music Garden and Sycamore Grove were also well attended. Sadly a group of eucalyptus in the grove failed to survive the hard winter of 1890 and had to be replaced by specimens of *Ailanthis*, the Tree of Heaven from China.

Queen Victoria photographed outside the Indian Pavilion when she visited the Royal Naval Exhibition at Chelsea .

Another import around this time was the Indian Pavilion, purchased from the Peninsular and Orient Steamship Company for which it had been designed by the architect to the Imperial Institute, T E Collcutt, for the Royal Naval Exhibition at Chelsea in 1891. It was re-assembled near the Music Garden and, until it was demolished in 1963 to make way for the Congress Theatre, it served as dressing rooms and as the Devonshire Lawns Tea Chalet.

2

SPORTS AND PASTIMES

The 'healthful sports of Cricket, Lawn Tennis, Racquets and Roller Skating' together with athletics, cycling and croquet were flourishing in Devonshire Park at the turn of the century.

Among the events that received a large amount of local support, as well as proving an attraction to visitors, were the annual Amateur Athletic Sports, pictured right, first held there in August 1874.

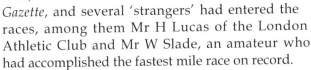

On that occasion the weather was delightfully fine, said the *Eastbourne Gazette*, and several 'strangers' had entered the races, among them Mr H Lucas of the London Athletic Club and Mr W Slade, an amateur who had accomplished the fastest mile race on record.

'In the half mile he acquitted himself in a way quite consistent with his reputation but Lucas was beaten easily by Mr E G Jeffery in the 100 yards race.'

There was local interest, too, in the new sport of bicycle racing. Before H J Lawson patented the Safety Bicycle and brought the rider nearer the ground, the ordinary or penny farthing with a 60-inch front wheel and a rear wheel of about 18 inches, was the machine on which the intrepid bicyclists careered round the park perimeter. By the 1900s when the

Competitors, supported on their penny farthings, watch for the starter's flag at
one of the cycle races held in the park in the mid 1870s.

Eastbourne Bicycle Club, the Eastbourne Bachelors' Cycle Club and the Eastbourne Cycle and Athletic Club were holding their race meetings in the park, back and front wheels were down to 28inches.

The Devonshire Park Cycle Academy, housed in a miniature temple at the beginning of the Broad Walk, had opened in 1896. It offered 'lessons to ladies visiting Eastbourne and desirous to acquire the most necessary art of wheeling in correct style.'

Croquet was out of fashion. There had been so little interest in playing the game on the lawns set out for it that they were turned into courts for the increasingly popular game of lawn tennis. Much to the annoyance of the George F Chambers, 'of the Inner Temple, Barrister-at-Law'. He expressed his disapproval in his highly personal *Old Memories of Eastbourne in Victorian Times*, published in 1910:

> 'Croquet was much played in East-bourne thirty years ago but when the disease of Lawn Tennis broke out and raged as an epidemic, Croquet went under for many years.'

Interest in the game revived in the 1890s when the rules were revised, the hoops narrowed, the settings improved and a national Croquet Association formed. Soon tournaments were being held all over the country. The first in Eastbourne was in 1896 and by the season of 1904 it had ousted cricket from the calendar of events as the brochure for that year explains:

> 'It was not without regret that, in view of the the growth and increasing demands of modern croquet the management of the Devonshire Park decided to omit cricket from the list of park games for, at all events, the present Season. There were, however, certain drawbacks attaching to the pursuit of the 'national game' in so limited an area, and it is hoped that the wisdom of the present course will be made manifest by the use made by Croquet players of the largely increased extent of lawns now placed at their disposal.'

There had been headaches from the outset over cricket, engendered perhaps by the old Eastbourne club losing its pitch to housing before arrangements for an alternative site had been discussed with its officers. An angry 'Old Cricketer' writing from London on December 8 1873 to the editor of the *Eastbourne Chronicle*, suggested the Duke should have said to his agent:

> 'When you turn cricketers out again give them a year's notice, and arrange that if I am going to build the new cricket ground it shall be commenced immediately after the season, and that all necessary drains shall be made long

beforehand, and that all arrangements shall be made for foundations being commenced on the building ground, and the natural soil being carted from building ground to the new site of cricket ground.'

An indication that cricket was on its way out of the park was given in the 1891 when important cricket fixtures were restricted to the month of August – 'when the greater influx of visitors takes places, many of them desirous of "wielding the willow" on a classic ground, rich in the memories of many a well fought fight', says the brochure for that year.

The charges for croquet were the same as for tennis – two shillings an hour in the morning, three shillings an hour in the afternoon. And subscribers wishing to give a garden party could book one or more courts on the Upper Lawn and have refreshments supplied to their guests from one of the Swiss chalets.

The management committee catered for the cultured and those with only a slight interest in participation and spectator sports, with outdoor concerts, illuminated fetes and firework displays.

What started the whole town talking in June 1895 was the balloon that went up at the Fancy Fair in aid of the Eastbourne Voluntary School's Extension Fund. The Carnation Balloon, filled with gas by a canvas hose from a nearby main, was secured to the ground by a winch.

Fifteen minute rides to a height of 1,000ft were well worth the fee charged, said the *Eastbourne Gazette* reporter, who was apparently accompanied by a photographer for an aerial photograph of the Winter Garden appeared in the following year's *Eastbourne Guide.*

The fair, which was opened by the Duchess of Devonshire, had nineteen stalls and several sideshows and produced a handsome profit of £1,245. 'A good and satisfactory result for a town with a population which then only amounted to somewhere about 30,000', commented George Chambers in his *Old Memories. . .*

Another first that year was the Workmen's Exhibition – much on the lines of a modern craft fair, except that this one included cigar making among the glass blowing, pottery and model making displays. It occupied both the Floral Hall and the Pavilion and its object, according to the official prospectus, was 'to afford Eastbourne workpeople and employers an opportunity of showing their ability to execute useful and ornamental works in the various handicrafts and to compete with the larger industrial centres.'

There was more and more music. The municipal orchestra, conducted by Theo Ward, gave two or three evening concerts weekly in the Floral Hall, and a Saturday night programme which included a 'vocalist or other entertainer' as well as playing for the roller skating assemblies. The Devonshire Park Grand Orchestra always ended the season with a Grand Concert – and none were grander than the one in 1906 when Norfolk Megone's fifty four instrumentalists were joined by the Band of the Coldstream Guards, the Band of the 2nd Sussex R G A Volunteers, the pipers of the Scots Guards plus the municipal orchestra and an unnamed military band.

Next door at the Devonshire Park Theatre, structural alterations had increased the size of the pit area by fifty per cent, extended the saloon bar, improved the ventilation and installed central heating. The two tiers of balconies, which formerly only extended across the end of the theatre, were carried round to the sides and 'handsome private boxes with imposing facades introduced' says the 1904 prospectus. Emergencies exits, into the park and into the street, were added and a large foyer built at dress circle level 'commanding a comprehensive and charming view of the grounds'. It was fitted with upholstered settees, seats and tables and at one end there was a buffet for the service of light refreshments.

The proscnium was totally rebuilt. Over the front it had a bust of Shakespeare, flanked by angels, and prominently lettered above the arch was a line from Hamlet's advice to the players:

'To hold as 'twere the mirror up to Nature'.

The act drop, of a beautiful lake scene in Switzerland was, says the prospectus, 'the work of Mr Richard Douglas, the well known scenic artist.'

3

EVERYONE FOR TENNIS

In the second half of the nineteenth century various versions of tennis were introduced, usually by retired Army officers, to the lawns of the cricket clubs of which they were members. In 1873 Major Walter Wingfield went so far as to patent his version of the game under the name of Sphairistike. It was played on an hour glass shaped court and the package deal he offered for six guineas included a net, two rackets, a dozen 'rubber cored and flannel covered' balls and a book of rather querky rules. For example there was no limit to the number of serves each player could make; no allowance for double faults; only servers could score a point in the fifteen point game; and if they lost the rally the service changed sides.

Not surprisingly his customers were confused and in 1875 Marylebone Cricket Club was asked by puzzled would-be players to advise on how the new game should be played. However, the Original Standardised Rules for Lawn Tennis it issued were not much of an improvement and the All England Croquet and Lawn Tennis Club set up its own committee in 1877 to sort matters out. The rules it produced for the first tournament at Wimbledon, which ran from July 9 to 16, 1877 – with a mid weekend break for the Eton v Harrow match – are, apart from a few minor changes, the same as those in force today.

The courts in Devonshire Park were laid out to the Wimbledon pattern. They were rectangular rather than hourglass in shape; measured 26ft by 9ft (8m by 2.76m); and the net, by F H Ayres, a firm which became a leading manufacturer of tennis equipment, was 39inches (1m) high at the middle, and supported by 5ft high posts planted a yard outside the court. They could be hired from 10am to 7pm on weekdays from the start of the 1880 season and balls were included in the charge of 1s 6d for singles court and two shillings for doubles in the mornings and two shillings for singles and three shillings for doubles in the afternoons. The booking hall was in one of the Swiss Chalets where dressing rooms and private lockers could be booked by the week or the month.

In June the following year the *Eastbourne Gazette* informed its readers that the lawn tennis courts were daily patronised by lovers of the game. Two months later it reported that a lawn tennis tournament was in progress and had 'excited great interest and is attentively watched by a large number of spectators. The pastime is in high favour and an additional charm is lent to it when played on the splendid ground of the Park.'

It ran from August 15 to 22 and appears to have been the first tennis tournament to be held in Devonshire Park. Mr G M Hill beat Mr W C Taylor in the final of the Gentlemen's singles and he and the winners of the Gentlemen's doubles and of the Ladies and Gentlemen's doubles received prizes of 'silver cups and ornamental articles of plate' from Mrs J L Hawkins.

A week later there was another tournament, this time a gentlemen's handicap event for which there were thirty two entries and the prize was a silver cup, worth five guineas, presented by Robert Insoll, chairman of the Devonshire Park and Baths Company. It was won by Mr E Cloete with Mr E J Avory as the runner up.

There was a bigger and better one to come. 'A Lawn tennis tournament which from the magnificence of the first prize, which will become the actual property of the winner, may be looked on as the chief of the contests played in Devonshire Park,' announced the *Eastbourne Gazette*.

'The massive silver cup, valued at fifty guineas, is one of the very finest we have seen.'

On September 14 1881 it devoted a third of a column to the tournament, much of it extolling the economic advantages of tennis to the town:

'It has been urged against the Devonshire Park that its prices preclude the general public from participating in its advantages but it must be remembered that the Park has among its chief patrons people who can well afford and are satisfied to pay the prices of admission and these are the very people who by their stay in Eastbourne most benefit the town in a financial way. The tournament which has been organised is a piece with the usual enterprise of the Park Company...
'During the progress of the tournament private games were not interfered with and those ladies and gentlemen who were desirous of amusing themselves at the popular sport invented by Colonel Wingfield had ample scope to do so.'

Four courts were in play throughout the fortnight and there was sunshine from the opening day to the final tie in which E Lubbock beat R W Badell in straight sets, 6-4, 6-2, 6-0. The winner received the fifty guinea trophy from the hands of Mrs L Famin, the wife of a member of the organising committee.

Was this the first South of England Championship? The programme of the tournament that began on September 12 1912, the cover of which is pictured right, is for 'the twenty-ninth annual meeting', suggesting a start date of 1882.

Certainly there was a 'grand lawn tennis tournament watched by a large throng' from August 30 1882. The Park Company

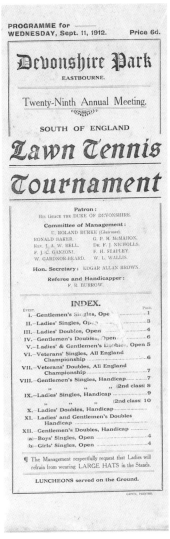

PROGRAMME for ————
WEDNESDAY, Sept. 11, 1912.   Price 6d.

Devonshire Park
EASTBOURNE.

Twenty-Ninth Annual Meeting.

SOUTH OF ENGLAND

Lawn Tennis
Tournament

Patron:
His Grace the DUKE OF DEVONSHIRE.

Committee of Management:
E. ROLAND BURKE (Chairman).
RONALD BAKER.   G. P. R. McMAHON.
Rev. J. A. W. BELL.   Dr. F. J. NICHOLLS.
F. J. C. GANZONI.   F. H. STAPLEY.
W. GARDNOR-BEARD.   W. L. WALLIS.

Hon. Secretary: EDGAR ALLAN BROWN.

Referee and Handicapper:
F. R. BURROW.

INDEX.

¶ The Management respectfully request that Ladies will refrain from wearing LARGE HATS in the Stands.

LUNCHEONS served on the Ground.

CAPON, PRINTER.

FIRST LAWN TENNIS TOURNAMENT, DEVONSHIRE PARK.
: SEPTEMBER, 1881. :
(Gentlemens Singles,)
BADDELL   v   LUBBOCK
WINNERS

directors had put up two cups for competition, one worth thirty guineas, the other twenty guineas. Was this because the previous year's top prize of a fifty guinea cup had become the property of the victorious Mr Lubbock?

It was wet and windy throughout the week and on Friday no play was possible. In Saturday's men's singles final R Williams beat W C Taylor 8-6, 6-2, 6-3. 'An instantaneous group was taken by Mr Lavis of the final heat' said the *Eastbourne Gazette*.

Is the picture above the one referred to, in spite of the inscription on it? Are the spectators sheltering under umbrellas from the rain or protecting themselves from the sun's rays with their parasols? It is hard to tell.

A date that is certain is 1885. In that year a ladies' singles was added to the championships and the title was won by Blanche Bingley, a player with a forehand that was formidable even by modern standards. In those

24

days of genteel stroke play it gained for her eleven Eastbourne titles and six Wimbledon championships. Most of her triumphs were as Mrs G W Hillyard, for in 1887 she married Commander Hillyard who later became secretary of the All England Tennis and Croquet Club.

Five more years were to pass before the women's singles winner at Eastbourne was to receive a trophy of equivalent value to that presented to her male counterpart. The Ladies' Cup was presented by the Duchess of Devonshire in 1900 and the first recipient was Miss M Wilson.

Not all the early tournaments were formally organised affairs. Eighteen gentlemen entered the 'private singlehanded lawn tennis tournament' which started on July 27 1882. Perhaps they were playing a version Spairistike for the prize of a racquet was won by G H Swinstead by the unusual score of '11 games to set'.

Or were they playing Hildegarde? This new game was described by the *Eastbourne Gazette* in July 1883 as 'a form of cricket combined with baseball with a suggestion of football and adapted to the use and strength of women'.

Was the newspaper being serious when it declared:

'Just when Lawn Tennis has attained a popularity quite unprecedented, entirely supplanting croquet and even boldly daring to bid for popularity with our time-honoured game of cricket, another rival has appeared on the field which, like Lawn Tennis, combines athletics and amusement and is suited for both sexes. This new game is called Hildegarde . . .'

4

THE BOROUGH BUY-OUT

Eastbourne Corporation made the first of a series of attempts to buy the park from the Devonshire Park and Baths Company in 1897. It came to nothing as the enterprise was making a profit and the shareholders were satisfied. However, by 1911, the year Eastbourne achieved borough status, they were not so satisfied. The previous season had been disastrous. The death of King Edward VII on May 6 had affected attendances at all types of entertainment throughout the country and, in the south particularly, outdoor events were further blighted by weeks of cold, wet weather.

There had also been some little local difficulties. It must have seemed a good idea, at the time the decision was taken, to close the Floral Hall during the summer months so a large stage could be built, and arrange for all the orchestral concerts to be held out of doors.

However the hoped-for idyll of hundreds of music lovers relaxing in deck chairs and listening to the works of the great composers on warm summer evenings in the Sycamore

The concert stand in its sylvan setting.

Grove rarely materialised. The majority of the concerts were rained off – or cancelled before a note was played because of the cold. Another blow was the decision of the ninth Duke, heavily beset by death duties, to disband the private orchestra founded by the seventh Duke.

This time it was the company which approached the council with the offer of a package deal – the baths, the Floral Hall, the theatre, the racquet court, the public bar in Compton Street, the manager's house, the Pavilion and eight shops in Carlisle Road for £110,655. A money back offer from the ninth Duke, who as the major shareholder would receive £23,085 from the sale, reduced the amount payable by £10,000.

The council was keen and members agreed to promote the necessary Bill in Parliament to confirm the transaction.

Eastbourne ratepayers, encouraged by the Lord's Day Observance Society and the United Temperance Council, were not so keen. They expressed strong disapproval of the Sunday concerts that had been started by the Devonshire Park and Baths Company and of the council holding a liquor licence. Letters and petitions flew back and forth, speeches for and against were delivered, but Eastbournians were adamant. Even the ninth Duke's offer of the interest on the balance of his holding to meet any annual shortfall from the park enterprise and the council's promise to sell the Compton Street pub and hold only a six day licence for the park restaurant failed to persuade them. In a poll taken on 13 February 1913 the majority against the purchase was 423 and the Bill was withdrawn.

Eight months later the buy-for-the-borough lobby tried again and presented the council with a petition with 3,485 signastures asking it to re-introduce the Bill for the acquisition of park. The opposition replied with a petition against the purchase signed by 3,152 people. As there were more for than against the Bill was again deposited – and again withdrawn when a poll of electors on February 3 1914 produced a majority of 695 against. With the outbreak of war in August all purchase plans were set aside. Instead the borough council disbanded the Eastbourne Municipal Orchestra and persuaded the directors of the Devonshire Park Company to share the cost of supplying a 'good orchestra' to play in the park and a military band to play on the sea front at suitable times all the year round.

Listening to the music and savouring the peace of the park were soldiers

Tea cups, and a tea pot, at the ready in the Welcome Hut of Summerdown Convalescent Hospital.

from the Summerdown Convalescent Military Camp in their blue uniforms. It had been opened early in 1915, in an area bounded by the present Old Camp Road, Pashley Road and Compton Drive, for men recovering from wounds received on the Western Front. Later it also accommodated those from the Dardanelles campaign.

The hutted camp had its own gymnasium/theatre, billiards room, shooting gallery, skittle alley and a Welcome Hut, staffed by female volunteers who took pride in providing meals twenty four hours a day seven days a week. Eastbourne's welcome to the wounded was not confined to the camp. All the town's leisure facilities were open to them and, as their recovery progressed, they were able to take advantage of the activities on offer in Devonshire Park and roller skate, play bowls, tennis, croquet and cricket.

It was not until 1923 that yet another draft Parliamentary Bill for the purchase of the park was prepared – and dropped when a poll of electors produced an astounding 4,490 against.

The company then offered to sell piecemeal what it could not unload as a package. The swimming baths were acquired by the council for £15,000 in November 1924 and six years later it paid £30,000 for the Floral Hall, Pavilion, manager's house and outside skating rink. At the same time it agreed to buy the grounds for an additional £25,000 when the company was prepared to sell them.

The council decided not to lease the property it had acquired but instead appointed a management committee to run it and the entertainments that would be provided. The liquor licence problems were sorted out by a simple division of responsibility. The council would hold the licence for the Winter Garden, Floral Hall and Tea Lounge, and the company for the pub and the Indian Pavilion.

The buy-out received royal recognition on June 30 1931 when the Prince of Wales came by air from Windsor, landed at the flying ground

As the Prince of Wales' red Rolls Royce drove under a triumphal arch of fishing boats and nets Police Constable Maurice Clayton gives a possibly inadvertent display of rough riding.

in Kings Drive, was driven in a red Rolls Royce to the town hall, and unveiled a tablet recording the purchase of the park.

It was his only official visit to Eastbourne and it was a busy one. He inspected various military detachments, laid wreaths at the war memorial, was shown round two housing estates, the fishing and lifeboat station and given a civic lunch at the Grand Hotel. The menu for the occasion included caviar or melon, poached salmon, chicken en cocotte with peas and new potatoes, asparagus, a peach and strawberry pudding and cheese and biscuits. After it the prince laid the foundation stone of a new wing at the Princess Alice Hospital, had tea at Eastbourne College and flew home to Windsor in his monoplane.

In 1946, almost fifty years after making its first bid for the park, the council received the eight acres of grounds from the parent company, which had ceased trading in that year, and one of the most disrupted sales of the century was finally completed.

In 1957 the freehold of the Devonshire Park Theatre and of the old racquets court was bought by the borough for £33,750, bringing the total bill to £103,750.

5

1919 – A SEASON OF FIRSTS

Competitive tennis returned to the park in July 1919 with the first tie since the war for the Dwight Davis Cup, a rose bowl which had become the 'ashes' of international lawn tennis since it was presented in 1907 by Harvard student Dwight F Davis 'to promote a sporting competition where the best players from the growing family of tennis nations in the world could compete in a convivial atmosphere'.

The British Isles faced South Africa at Eastbourne in the initial round of the preliminary competition. The winner would go on to meet either Belgium or France – there were only four nations in the draw that year – to see who would challenge the holders, Australasia.

The Devonshire Park was well prepared. Two substantial stands had been put up overlooking the principal courts, the turf was in perfect condition, famous players had been booked to give exhibition matches and a varied programme of indoor entertainment had been arranged, including a grand concert in the Winter Garden featuring the renowned contralto, Madame Clara Butt.

Although the light was bad and rain always threatened the British Isles won the two singles matches played on the Friday, Major T M Mavrogordato beating Lieutenant L Raymond 1-6, 7-5, 2-6, 8-6, 6-1 and Lt Col A R F Kingscote beating Lieut G H Dodd in straight sets, 6-3, 6-3, 6-2. Saturday was doubles day, the weather was kinder and the stands were packed for what turned out to be a nerve-tingling match. The team captain, H Roper Barrett, who played in the first Davis Cup contest in Boston, was making his last appearance in a home tie. He was partnered by Algernon Kingscote against South Africans Dodd and H Aitken. The

31

British pair were two games down, then won three in succession, before eventually taking the first set 7-5. It was the same in the second set. The South Africans established a 5-2 lead before their opponents caught and passed them, winning 9-7 and going on the secure the final set 6-3.

Honours were shared in the last two singles matches, Mavrogordato going down to Dodd 9-7, 7-5, 3-6, 4-6, 7-5. The British Isles team went on to beat the winners of the Belgium v France tie and make the long sea trip to Sydney where they failed to capture the cup from Australia.

The first Professional Lawn Tennis Championship of Great Britain, an event which proved to be a popular addition to the Eastbourne tennis season, both before and after the Second World War, was held in August 1919 and the winner was C Hierons.

Dan Maskell in action in the Professional Championships.

From 1920 to 1927, with the exception of 1924, the Queen's Club coach C R Read was the winner. He was in his fifties when Dan Maskell, who was to become the voice of tennis to generations of listeners to BBC Wimbledon commentaries took the singles title from him and kept it up to the Second World War, with the exception of 1937 when it was won by his doubles partner T C Jeffery. Maskell continued his winning ways when the championship was resumed in 1946, but as 'D Maskell O.B.E.' an honour he received for his services to British tennis.

In September the South of England Lawn Tennis Tournament, which, said the *Eastbourne Herald,* was 'emphatically the event of the season, regarded either socially or recreationally', was back in business after a six year gap. There were no fewer than 760 entries, including such top names of the day as ex King Manoel of Spain; Mrs Lambert Chambers (formerly Dolly Douglas) a seven times Wimbledon winner; doubles champion M J G Ritchie; and nineteen year old South African Brian Norton who went on to win the 1921 All Comers final and was runner up to the great Bill Tilden in the last Wimbledon Challenge Round.

Also there was Elizabeth Ryan, fresh from her Wimbledon doubles triumph partnered by Suzanne Lenglen, then at the start of her fabulous tennis career. Elizabeth won the ladies singles and, partnered at Eastbourne by Mrs Lambert Chambers, collected the doubles title as well. Major Mavrogordato, this time at Devonshire Park on his own account rather than as a Davis Cup team player, took the men's singles title.

During the tournament a total of 1,250 matches were played and the *Daily Telegraph* special correspondent congratulated the management on completing all the level events before the sun had fallen below the giant stands on Saturday. He went on:

'. . . there has been no pre-war Eastbourne tournament in my fairly long memory at which the winners were identified so punctually, and at which the committee (and all the old hands were at work again after a lapse of six years), strove so valiantly'.

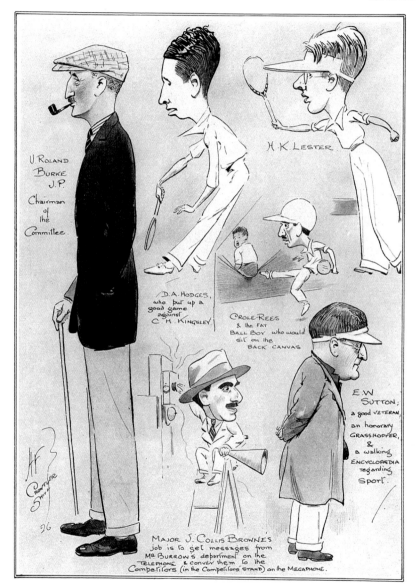

"COURT" CARICATURES FROM THE SOUTH OF ENGLAND CHAMPIONSHIPS.

ONE OF THE LAST GRASS · COURT TOURNAMENTS : EASTBOURNE LAWN · TENNIS PERSONALITIES.

6

THE GARDEN PARTY YEARS

A leisurely garden party atmosphere pervaded the competitive tennis scene at Devonshire Park in the years between the wars. The courts had their characters among the officials as well as the players and they were of sufficient prominence to merit a page of caricatures in *The Sketch* of 1926. The megaphone method adopted by Major J Collis-Browne of getting the players from their stand on to the courts came in for criticism from Stanley Doust, one of the contestants in the 40th annual South of England Championships, a couple of years later.

'The calling of names through megaphones makes an unholy din', he complained to a reporter. 'At Eastbourne the calling of names goes on throughout the day and often affects – as it did in this tournament – the players to such an extent that they lose points and even matches because of the noise . . .'

He suggested that instead of calling all players for 10.30am, apart from those on the '10 o'clock list' posted up the night before, they should be given a schedule of the day's play.

'If players knew the night before what matches were to be played in the morning and at noon what matches were to be played in the afternoon it would obviate the incessant calling out of names', he argued.

Referee and handicapper F R Burrow, who was also the referee at Wimbledon and a personality to be reckoned with in interwar years tennis, did not agree. 'In theory a perfect system, in practice impracticable at Eastbourne where time is limited,' he said. 'Here players are engaged in one, two and three matches a day and no one can say how long a match is going to last.'

The *Eastbourne Gazette* devoted many column inches to the social and fashion side of Tennis Week. Each year Miss Gossip, the pseudonym used by Mrs Russell Goggs, a reporter who wielded as much power in

Centre court action at the South of England Championships in the garden party days.

the drawing rooms of Eastbourne as Hedda Hopper did among the studios of Hollywood, described the dresses, the parties and what the players were wearing.

In 1933, for the first time, a woman was seen on the court in shorts. In her account of this fashion first Miss Gossip does not express approval or disapproval but leaves it to the wearer to argue their advantages:

> 'Once you have worn them you never want to wear a frock again! Miss Freda James was referring to the garments which seemed to provide the general topic of conversation on Monday and almost created more interest than the play or the players.
>
> 'In America, she says, everyone wears shorts and so no one is conspicuous. They give you so much more liberty than skirts and make running so easy. If Helen Jacobs and other players had come I am sure they would have worn them.

Freda James was the only member of the Wightman Cup team able to enter the 45th South of England Championships. 'This is my fourth year here, I would not have missed the Eastbourne tournament for anything', she said.

Her one success of the week was as partner to V G Kirby, winner of all three men's titles, in the mixed doubles. He wore long trousers – she wore her shorts.

Miss Gossip went on to tell her readers that:

'Tea at the Indian Pavilion has become an institution. Many smart little parties were made up on Monday afternoon and everything was well done for the 45th annual championships'.

Advertisements for the Indian Pavilion Tea Lounge (Fully Licensed) offered: 'Dainty teas at moderate prices. Cakes, Scones etc made on the premises by an experienced lady confectioner'.

Before, or after, a dainty tea visitors could play two rounds of Tom Thumb golf on the nine hole course for sixpence or play squash for forty minutes in 'two of the most up-to-date standard size courts with modern changing rooms with hot and cold baths and showers' at a cost of 1s 6d

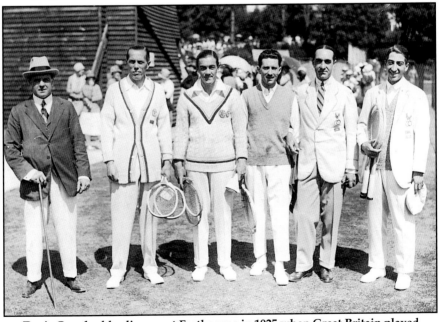

Davis Cup doubles line up at Eastbourne in 1925 when Great Britain played France. L to r: H Roper Barrett, non playing captain of the home team; L A Godfree; J D P Wheatley; J Brugnon; Max Decugis; and R Lacoste.

37

Bunny Austin in play against Donald Budge the the 1936 Davis Cup tie against the USA.

per player.

These new courts had been built the previous year on the site of the Devonshire Park bandstand which had become surplus to requirements when the borough council acquired the Redoubt in 1931 and converted this fort, built in the 1790s to defend the coast against Napoleon's threatened invasion, into a music garden with a bigger bandstand.

Davis Cup ties continued to bring more big names to Eastbourne. In 1927, when South Africa played France and went on to win the cup, the French team included Jean Borotra, the 'bounding Basque' so loved by Wimbledon Centre Court crowds, and two other Wimbledon winners, Rene Lacoste and Henri Cochet. Lacoste had been at the park two years previously when Great Britain met France.

A smash from Perry as he works his way to victory against Fujikura.

Between 1933 and 1936 Fred Perry and 'Bunny' Austin were the 'names' in the games that won Great Britain the Davis Cup four years in succession. The 1933 tie at Eastbourne against Italy started with the shock defeat of Perry in the singles by the ambidextrous G de Stefani but this was his country's only victory in the matches played.

On the same courts, a week later, Perry, Austin, G P Hughes and H G N Lee defeated Czechoslovakia in the European zone semi final.

Perry was back at the park the following year to play in an international 'friendly' match between Great Britain and Japan. This time he

The Sussex Ladies who won the inter county championship in 1925 were at Eastbourne's first County Week in 1927. They are, l to r: Mrs Watson, Miss J Brown, Mrs Milton, Miss E Tyrell, Miss Rodocanachi and Miss Tripp.

won his singles against J Fujikura 6-1, 2-6, 6-4, 10-8.

The year 1927 also saw the first County Week at Eastbourne – another event that brought star players to Devonshire Park and enthusiastic crowds of spectators to watch them play.

Inter County Championships on grass for men had been introduced by the Lawn Tennis Association in 1895 and in 1899 a Ladies Inter County Cup competition was added. The format changed over the years but by 1925 the pattern for County Week, much as it is today, was established. There were thirty four men's teams and thirty six women's teams and the counties were placed, by merit, into six groups, each group playing at a fixed base.

In 1925 Sussex Ladies, playing in Group 1 at Roehampton, became the county champions for the first – and so far only– time. Surrey were the winners in the Group 1 Ladies' first year at Eastbourne, defeating teams from Durham, East of Scotland, Middlesex, Sussex and Warwickshire.

The 1936 British Junior Lawn Tennis Champion, Gem Hoahing, spent the entire summer of 1938 in Eastbourne with her parents, joined the tennis club at the park and played regularly for its first team. Miss Gossip had talent spotted her at the 45th South of England Championships:

'The little Chinese girl, Gem Hoahing, who won the junior challenge cup at

Sandown, is twelve but looks younger. She was entered by her parents at the last moment in the women's singles and met Wisard and lost.'

Gem had joined the Devonshire Park Lawn Tennis Club, one of the clubs formed in the 1880s by the Devonshire Park and Baths Company to oversee a specific sport in the park. It originally had courts on the Upper Lawn and, as it increased in prestige, it was allocated six courts each month for its own exclusive use. They were screened with canvas and clearly marked 'For Members Only'.

It was not all that easy to become a member, as today's president of the Devonshire Park Lawn Tennis Club, Ted Robins, discovered when he moved to Eastbourne in 1935 and opened a mens' wear shop in Grove Road.

'They turned me down because I was in trade', he said. 'However, the following year I was invited to have a game with some important local players, including International player, Tim Horn. After they had seen the quality of my tennis we had tea in the Indian Pavilion and I was told they would bend the rules in my case.'

Ted, now in his nineties, remembers that tea-time offer, and his response to it, well. He imposed a condition. Membership must also be extended to his business partner, Reginald Edwards, who was keen but only an average player.

'They agreed to take us both and we were the first "in trade" to be admitted,' he said. 'In 1937 the club which had rejected me asked me to be its captain. I refused, until after the war when the club had abandoned its stuffy social barriers.'

Ted, a member of the International Club of Great Britain, represented his country in the 45 and Over Dubler Cup competition in Norway. 'We played on the slowest hard courts I have ever experienced - it was like playing on sand. No wonder we lost,' he recalled. 'They were nothing like the beautiful hard courts we used to have in Devonshire Park. When I was living away from Eastbourne for a time I would travel down with my son at weekends specifically to play on them.'

From 1935 until they finished in 1974 Ted was a regular competitor in the South of England Championships and had some experience of the confusion caused by the system of handicap tennis played before the war. He won the All England Veterans' Championship a record thirteen times and gave a trophy, the Perpetual Challenge Cup, to replace the one he had so repeatedly won. 'When the event was no longer held I asked for it back,' he said. 'It is now among my treasured mementoes, together with the original silver salver signed, in their own handwriting, by all the players who have won it.'

○ ○ ○

7

ANOTHER WAR – AND ITS AFTERMATH

There was no indication, in that golden summer of 1939, that the garden party in the park was coming to an end. Children played, unafraid and unthreatened, on the green painted wood and metal slides, swings, roundabouts and seesaws provided for them in the Children's Corner. Sessions in the sea water swimming baths were well patronised, there were the usual tea dances in the Winter Garden, the *Fols de Rols* was the show for the season in the Floral Hall, at the Devonshire Park Theatre new plays were having their prior to London try outs, there was the sound of racket on ball from the tennis courts, the click of croquet mallets from the upper lawn . . .

However, in the sea front hotels the holiday season was ending earlier than usual. On Saturday, September 2 their foyers were full of people with suitcases waiting for taxis to take them to the station, or to be collected by car. Hundreds of bookings had been cancelled as the world waited apprehensively for Germany to respond to Britain's ultimatum and withdraw its troops from Poland and most of the nation was at home on the Sunday morning to hear Neville Chamberlain announce that the country was at war.

When, after the high drama of the 'false alarm' air raid warning that followed the prime minister's broadcast, nothing very exciting happened, Eastbourne settled down to distributing gas masks; coming to terms with the blackout; and getting back to business as usual.

Places of entertainment that had been closed by government decree reopened and the council's Winter Garden managing committee resumed its programme of celebrity concerts. A fatality, however, was the South of England Championships scheduled for the first two weeks of September. The event had coincided with the initial panic period when devastating air raids were expected hourly and it was not considered sensible to allow crowds to congregate.

In the Phoney War that preceded the fall of France there was the belief that, as in the 1914-18 war, Eastbourne would continue to flourish as a holiday resort. Strange's *Popular Guide for Eastbourne* of 1941 obviously expected it to, as this laudatory piece on the park implies:

'Devonshire Park is perhaps the most unique institution of its kind in England, possessing as it does a park of some acres, the Floral Hall, a concert hall, ballroom, lecture room and indoor and outdoor skating rink, tea lounge, well appointed reading and writing rooms replete with all newspapers and magazines, tennis pavilion, racquets court, swimming baths, private baths and a theatre which is so tastefully decorated and well appointed that it would be no exaggeration to say that it is unequalled on the South Coast.

The beautiful grounds of the Park afford exceptional facilities to those interested in the popular pastime of tennis and it is very rare indeed (with the exception of wet days) that one can enter the grounds and see less than a dozen or so courts engaged by the devotess of this game. Matches between the local team and the universities and other well known lawn tennis clubs are a frequent occurrence and in the month of September the tennis season culminates with the South of England Lawn Tennis Championship meeting. This meeting is famous worldwide, gathering together as it does all the first class European and Colonial exponents of the game.'

Had no one told the *Popular Guide* that there was a war on?

In the summer of 1940 Eastbournians soon became aware that there was. On Sunday, July 12, as the Luftwaffe started to soften up British resistance in preparation for invasion, the first bombs fell on the town, killing two people. The following day an order was made banning all visitors to Channel coast resorts. Sea front hotels were closed, beaches barricaded with barbed wire, sections cut out of the piers and pill boxes built on the promenades.

In August the borough council seriously considered closing down the whole Winter Garden complex for the duration but there were so many voices raised against the idea that it was decided to keep the Floral Hall open but close the cinema, which was then housed in the Pavilion on the upper level. This compromise was not appreciated by men of the First and Second Divisions of the Canadian Army who later on were billeted in the Winter Garden and scratched their initials on a pane of the glass wall of the Floral Hall. They would have liked a cinema on site.

By the spring of 1944 a total of 675 high explosives and 3,625 incendaries had rained down on the resort and caused more than 1,100 civilian casualties, 174 of them fatal. Some 475 houses were reduced to piles of rumble and a further 1,000 seriously damaged.

Devonshire Park was not damaged by enemy action but by neglect. All its able bodied gardeners and groundsmen had been called up with the result that trees and shrubs were untrimmed and its many specimen plants untended. Its buildings had not been maintained and there were deep cracks in the surface of the outdoor skating rink as no attempt had been made to protect it from the severe frosts of those wartime winters.

A discouraging report on the condition of the park was received by the borough council in July 1946 when the sale from the Devonshire Park and Baths Company was finally completed. The intention was to make it a centre for world class tennis and to re-establish Eastbourne as a holiday resort and conference town. But there were more pressing priorities. Damaged properties had to be repaired, new homes for heroes had to be built when there was a desparate shortage of materials of all kinds and ways had to be found through a minefield of licences, permits and quotas before one brick could be placed upon another. For the next five years all the council could do about the Winter Garden and the park it stood in was to talk .

The 'let's knock it down and start again from scratch' suggestion found favour with a number of members and the chief officers produced a plan for a conference centre not only on the Winter Garden site but also on the skating rink; the existing entrance to the park; and the Indian Pavilion, recently renamed the Devonshire Lawns restaurant. It came with the rider that it was 'impossible to proceed on the lines envisaged as the amount of money available to spend on the new building would not even cover the cost of providing the facilities currently available in the existing building'. In effect, 'cannot afford it'.

Fortunately the tennis was not held up by the talking. The work of restoring the courts to first class conditions was undertaken so successfully that Devonshire Park soon became the centre for competitions of the highest importance involving players of world class. One of the first of these events was the Professional Championships of Great Britain,

Ken Rosewall, who arrived on the British tennis scene from Australia with Lew Hoad in 1952, was three times runner up in the Wimbledon Mens' final.

with Dan Maskell continuing to win both singles and doubles. An international exhibition match in August 1954 featuring such greats as Fred Perry – for some reason representing the USA on this occasion – D Tregonning and P Cawthorne of Australia; Mohammed Aly of Egypt; and R Probst and K Pohmann of Germany.

Conditions were also improved for the increasing number of spectators with the provision of a covered stand erected in time for the 63rd South of England Championships in 1955. Seats in the stand could be reserved for the whole tournament for £1 7s 6d (137½p) or purchased daily for 5s 0d (25p). Ladies Final Day seats were 6s 0d (27½p) and it cost 7s 6d to watch the Mens' Final from the new stand.

Three years later the Slazenger Professional Lawn Tennis Tournament moved from Scarborough to Devonshire Park, bringing to its Trophy Rounds such famous players as Lew Hoad, Ken Rosewall, Tony Trabert and Pancho Segura.

The resumption of the Inter County Championships in 1947 brought the top names in British tennis to Eastbourne. The 1949 Middlesex women's team included ten Wimbledon players and Surrey was able to call on Geoff Paish, Gerry Oakley and Roger Becker. Until 1953, when eighteen courts were made available at Eastbourne for both championship groups, the men's and women's championships had been staged there on alternate years in County Week.

Both sexes suffered in 1960. A violent thunderstorm accompanied by torrential rain flooded the courts at Devonshire Park and the decision that gave Middlesex the men's championship was only obtained after Essex conceded the two final rubbers. An attempt had been made to decide the vital match on the hard courts at the Redoubt but bad light stopped play with Middlesex leading 4-3.

The second place in the women's championship also had to be decided at the Redoubt where Warwickshire, represented by Mrs Defford and Mrs Cheadley, beat Miss J Fulton and Mrs F Marsh of Yorkshire 7-5, 6-2.

8

ALL CHANGE FOR
OPEN TENNIS

As the austerity Fifties were succeeded by the Swinging Sixties the strain
on the council's coffers eased and in July 1961 the Chatsworth Estates
approved the plans for the long-awaited conference centre. On June 13
two years later, the 1,700 seater Congress Theatre opened with a gala
concert by the London Philharmonic Orchestra conducted by Sir Arthur
Bliss, Master of the Queen's Music. It had taken eighteen months to
build, cost some £2 million and was to win a national award from the
British Travel and Holiday Association which judged it to be the most
outstanding addition to Britain's tourist attractions that year. At about
the same time the Lawn Tennis Association was making complimentary
comments about the twenty or so grass and four hard courts in
Devonshire Park, even going so far as to describe them as 'some of the
best in the world.'

To the best courts came the best players, and the crowds to watch
them. The stands were packed on August 27 1963 for a professional exhibition match played by four former Wimbledon champions – Australians
Lew Hoad, Rod Laver; and Frank Sedgman and Peruvian Alejandro
Olmedo – the latter virtually unknown in international tennis until his
sensational victories when playing for the US in the Davis Cup Challenge
Round of 1958.

By the end of the decade top tennis was being played for money not
medals. The debate about Open tennis had been raging, with varying
degrees of intensity, since the mid Thirties. It ended in 1967 when the All
England Club staged an all-professional tournament at Wimbledon,

won, incidentally by Rod Laver. The following year the championships were open to both amateurs and professionals – and the rest of the world followed suit. Soon sponsors' names and logos were blazoned across programmes, on marquees and on the clothes and accoutrements of the players.

And these new sponsors were not necessarily directly associated with the sport. It was Green Shield, the company providing the retail trade with discount stamps for customers to collect and stick in books, who first sponsored the Junior Grass Court Championships of Great Britain, a new competition which started at Devonshire Park in 1970 and was a popular feature of the tennis season there until its demise twenty years later. It had competitions for ages from Eighteen and Under down to Twelve and Under and the first titleholders were Robin Drysdale, who beat John Feaver 6-4,10-8; and Lesley Charles who beat L Blanchford 7-5, 1-6, 6-4. The 1990 winners were J Barton and Shirli-Ann Siddall.

The following year, with Rothmans' backing, the South of England Championships became part of the Pepsi Grand Prix of Lawn Tennis – the biggest international tennis circuit of the day. It was controlled by the International Tennis Federation and its thirty six tournaments, which were open to both men and women, included Wimbledon, the US Open and the French Open.

Players who had competed regularly in these championships over the years found themselves playing alongside such tennis 'names' as Ken Rosewall, Fred Stolle, Bob Hewitt, Maria Bueno and Betty Stove – all anxious to get in as much grass court practice as they could in the run-up to Wimbledon. It was a bonus for Eastbourne spectators to see world class players in action and spot who was on match winning form but it was no new thing for a South of England champion to go on to triumph at the All-England club tournament. Laurie Doherty, younger of the famous brothers who dominated tennis between 1896 and 1907, was five times a Wimbledon winner; before him there was Wilfred Baddeley, South of England and Wimbledon champion from 1893 to 1896. Past Devonshire Park crowds basked in the reflected glory of Charlotte Sterry five Wimbledon wins and the seven notched up by Mrs Lambert Chambers.

Since 1971 the glory has been even greater. Among the seeds in the singles draw of the 1973 Rothmans South of England Championships was the Spanish left hander Manuel Orantes who was to win the US

The strong forehand of England's Mark Cox, helped him to a five set victory over Gonzalez in the British Hard Courts championships of 1968.

Open two years later, thrashing Jimmy Connors in the final; Britain's Mark Cox, who made tennis history when he became the first amateur to defeat a professional in an open tournament; and the Wimbledon title holder Andres Gimeno.

The first John Player tournament in 1974, with nearly £12,000 in prize money at stake, was combined with the eighty second – and last – South of England Championships. Virginia Wade, on her way to the final in which she was defeated by Chris Evert 5-7, 4-6, had a three set tussle with a young Czechoslovakian player, Martina Navratilova. She lost the first set 3-6, coasted to a 6-1 victory in the second, but had to battle for every point in the 6-4 decider. The following year Virginia won the Eastbourne Women's International Tournament, sponsored by the Lawn Tennis Association, defeating Billie Jean King 7-5, 4-6, 6-4. Headline news of that week, however, was the marriage of Evonne Goolagong to former Kent County player, Roger Cawley. During the tournament she had

Virginia Wade continued to collect titles during the decade – including the
Wimbledon Singles in its centenary year of 1977.

The two handed backhand is the stroke always associated with Chris Evert.
It bought her victory at Eastbourne and No 1 world ranking.

slipped away from Eastbourne for a quiet wedding without even telling her coach.

In 1977 came a high spot in the history of tennis at Devonshire Park. It was the chosen venue for the first staging in England of the Federation Cup, an event inaugurated in 1963 and involving thirty three countries. Bookings poured in from all parts of the world and to cope with the crowds an additional stand, seating 1,200, was put up. The holders, USA, represented by Chris Evert, Rosie Casals and Billie Jean King, beat the Australian team of Kerry Reid, Dianne Fromholtz and Wendy Turnbull to retain the title. The British team of Virginia Wade, Sue Barker, Linda Mottram and Michele Tyler fell to Australia in the semi-finals.

The decade ended with more change. The Devonshire Baths were closed and with them went the badminton courts. On December 13 1979 Chatsworth Estates approved plans for an airdome on the hard courts to house three badminton courts. It would be open all the year round and serve as an all-weather practice facility during the pre-Wimbledon Women's International Tennis Week.

Martina Navratilova.

9

MARTINA TRIUMPHS – AND A DAVIS CUP DRAMA

ONE player, more than any other, just by being there made the Eastbourne championships headline news throughout the world. Martina Navratilova, eleven times winner of the title, has a devoted on and off court following at Eastbourne. Her fans packed the stands whenever she was playing, and any social event she might possibly attend. Her first

appearance at Devonshire Park was in 1975, the year she opted to renounce her Czechoslovakian citizenship and settle in the United States. She won the singles title for the first time in 1978 – and again in 1982, 1983, 1984, 1985, and 1986. Partnered by Pam Shriver she collected the doubles title from 1981 to 1986 as well.

There was a momentary glitch in her run of victories in 1987. Helena Sukova of Czechoslovakia, who Martina had defeated in the two previous finals, was a third time lucky 7-6, 6-3 winner, but the situation was back to normal in 1988, and 1989, and 1990, and 1991. Martina unsuccessfully defended her Eastbourne title in 1994, her last year in singles competition, then went on to win her tenth Wimbledon.

Helena Sukova holds up the Pilkington Glass trophy.

Ballboys for the championships are girls from Cavendish School and Moira House School, in the LTA uniform colours of red shirts, navy blue skirts and white baseball caps.

The Hendon family, Nola, George and Eileen.

Two people who have also had much to do with the success of tennis at Devonshire Park, arrived in the days of Martina's triumphs.

George Hendon, now known to everyone as Eastbourne's 'Mr Tennis', directed his first tournament here in 1980. It was sponsored by BMW and won by Tracy Austin, an American teenager with a brace on her teeth. She won it the following year as well, also collecting her second US Open title before back problems and injuries forced her out of tennis. When the Lawn Tennis Association opened the doors to sponsorship in 1963 George was with Rothmans of Pall Mall, the first commercial concern to be allowed to be associated with a tennis tournament – the Kent championships at Beckenham.

However, by the time Rothmans sponsored its first Eastbourne tournament George had set up his own business consultancy and was there as a member of the Women's Professional Council, the organisation which ran the sport, representing the European Tournaments of the World Tour.

A chance meeting at Wimbledon with the then chairman, now president, of the Lawn Tennis Association, John Robbins, brought George into tournament administration. He was asked if he would like to run the British Hard Courts championships at Bournemouth and immediately said 'yes'. From there the Hendons came to Eastbourne where they operate as a family unit, his wife Eileen and daughter Nola taking personal care of the players individual needs and requirements and George with overall responsibility for the production of the courts, complete with 100 ballboys – who, in fact, are girls from Moira House and Cavendish Schools – and bringing together all the thousand and one things that pack the stands and pack the town in the week before Wimbledon.

The Lawn Tennis Association, in partnership with Eastbourne Borough Council and the commercial sponsor, run the championships through a committee of management which was until 1997 under the chairmanship of Austin Smith of the LTA. He has now handed

Ronald Cussons.

57

Winning smiles from Britain's Davis Cup team of (l to r) Buster Mottram, John Feaver, non-playing captain Paul Hutchins, John Lloyd, Roger Taylor and trainer Roger Becker after defeating Romania at Eastbourne in 1976.

over to Ian Hewitt. Overall reponsibility for the borough council's contribution has been in the hands of its Director of Tourism, Leisure and Amenities, Ronald Cussons, since 1986.

He came to Eastbourne from Bradford where, as Principal Leisure Officer, he had been involved with designing and building new leisure facilities such as theatres and sports venues. This experience was to come in handy years later when a fire, started by unknown arsonists on the night of November 13 1993, resulted in the biggest alteration to the appearance of Devonshire Park since Henry Currey's Winter Garden was built.

There was days of drama and destruction of a different kind in the 1980s. Eastbourne's Davis Cup connection had been maintained since the war and it was still proving a predominately lucky venue for the home team. Great Britain lost to Italy in 1950, Tony Mottram and Geoff Paish going down 2-3 in the first round of the European Zone competition; and to the same country in 1955 when Roger Becker, Tony Mottram,

Geoff Paish, Mike Davies and Bobby Wilson were beaten in the semi-final. It was a different story in 1962 when the home side had a 4-1 quarter final victory over Brazil; in 1976 when they beat Romania; and two years later when Buster Mottram, John and David Lloyd, Mark Cox and Richard Lewis beat Czechoslovakia 5-1 in the European Zone final.

The tie that Eastbourne will forever remember, not for the tennis but for the tension, apprehension and massive security that accompanied it, was the 1985 contest between Great Britain and Israel. There had never been anything like it before at Devonshire Park. Snipers were stationed on the roof of the Congress Theatre, their rifles trained on the centre court. Parking was not allowed anywhere in the vicinity and spectators had their bags searched every time they went in or out of the ground. Bad weather added to the problems and the tie – and its security – had to be transferred to the indoor courts at the Windmill Hill Tennis Centre, ten miles away at Herstmonceux. In spite of all this action and distraction the British team of Jeremy Bates, Stephen Shaw, John Lloyd and Colin Dowdeswell won the final of the European B competition by four rubbers to one.

Des O'Connor gives some informal coaching to the young and the very young at the Family Festival.

The weather which had upset the Davis Cup tie again caused disruption, and on a much more devastating scale, on October 16 1987. The hurricane force winds which wreaked havoc all through southern England, flattened many of the specimen trees and shrubs in Devonshire Park, damaged buildings and covered the courts with debris. The roof of the old North Stand took a lot of punishment and it was renewed in 1989 so it would conform to the provisions of the Safety at Sports Grounds Act.

Two years later a Family Festival of Tennis, with competitions for all age groups, was introduced to Eastbourne's tennis programme to fill the void caused by the removal to Nottingham of the National British Junior

Ann Jones.

Grass Courts Championships. The South of England Championships were revived, but for veteran players in particular age categories.

There were competitions for men over thirty five, over forty five, over fifty five, over sixty, and over sixty five and for women over forty, over fifty and over sixty. Both these events have proved hugely popular, both with the players and the spectators, and are still running today.

Since 1987 the Eastbourne championships have been refereed by Ann Jones, née Haydon, the first left-handed woman to win Wimbledon, which she did in 1969, defeating Billie Jean King in three sets.

Birmingham born Ann's first triumph on the international scene was in 1961 when she won the French title. She collected it again in 1966 and the following year was a runner-up at Wimbledon and in the US championships. The demands of motherhood – she has three children and wished to be with them as they grew up – reduced Ann's involvement in tournament tennis as a player but she did a great deal towards setting up and helping to develop the Women's International Tennis Association.

10

AFTER THE BLAZE – A NEW BUILDING

The centre court's North Stand was destroyed by fire on the night of Saturday, November 13, 1993. Three fire engines from Eastbourne and crews from Pevensey and Hailsham were quickly on the scene and twenty firefighters wearing breathing apparatus fought unsuccessfully to save the 70 year old wooden structure. At the height of the blaze flames whipped up by the gale force wind threatened houses in Blackwater Road and, as a

The North Stand after the fire.

The new West Stand was beginning to take shape by early March 1995.

The too-bright red telephone which stopped play on some of the outer courts.

precaution, their occupants were evacuated. On Sunday morning council officers moved in to assess the damage caused by the fire, believed to have been started under the seats of the stand by two youths seen entering the park around 9pm the previous evening.

The borough council had six months either to rebuild or replace the stand with a temporary structure for the 1994 Volkswagen Cup. It decided to rebuild and brought forward plans Director of Tourism Ronald Cussons had been considering for a new stadium with all the facilities for major international tournaments.

Work began almost at once one the foundations of the first phase of an ambitious £2.5 million development which would extend the centre and number one court by three metres to comply with International standards. A new West Stand with a state-of-the-art media centre; a hospitality area with private boxes and dining rooms overlooking the centre court; changing rooms for players on the two show courts and a tournament adminstration centre was to be built on the site of the old number one court and a new North Stand would replace the one damaged by the fire. Phase two, funded by the LTA, was to be a new East Stand to bring the centre court seating capacity up to 6,000 and a 1,500 seater stand for the new number one court.

The weather was not kind to the the builders, Wates Construction, that winter but in spite of far too much rain two new centre court stands were finished in time for the 1995 tournament, the first to be sponsored by Direct Line.

A very different Devonshire Park greeted the players and spectators. Attendants in blue and white uniforms manned the entrance gates; there were buildings where there had not been buildings before; and a confusion of trade tents and marquees. Behind the Congress Theatre there was a hospitality 'house' in the shape of Direct Line Insurance's logo – a bright red telephone – which proved too much of an eye catcher. It was so shiny that it reflected the June sunshine into the eyes of players on the outside courts. Play had to be halted and the offending phone wrapped in vast quantities of non-reflective material, leaving just the tip of its red chimney showing. Winner of the championship that year was France's Nathalie Tauziat who had been defeated in the third round in 1994 by winner, Meredith McGrath.

The Winter Garden had received a comprehensive facelift in the 1980s and its beautifully appointed Gold Room, formerly the Pavilion or even more formerly the concert hall, was chosen by the LTA for a centenary dinner for all the players involved in group one of the Inter-County Grass Court Championships.

This event, which was started in 1895, has been associated with

Eastbourne since 1927. Over the years the competition, now involving eighty eight teams from forty four counties, has built up a loyal following, many of whom made a point of taking their holidays to coincide with County Week at Eastbourne.

Another crowd pulling attraction that year was the Davis Cup Euro/African Zone tie between between Great Britain and Monaco.

Greg Rusedski and Tim Henman helped Great Britain to a 5-0 victory and made the day of the hundreds of schoolgirls who had packed into the park to see them.

Davis Cup team captain David Lloyd and Greg Rusedski.

Construction work started again the moment the season had finished and when World Number One Monica Seles arrived a week early to practice for the 1996 championships – which she won – a start had been made on phase two.

Monica was back the following year but failed the reach the final of one of the wettest championships on record. In the end the weather was, in effect, the winner. The tournament over-ran to the Sunday and, after a delayed start and several interruptions for rain, the singles finalists, Jana Novotna and Arantxa Sanchez Vicario, agreed to share the title.

It was still pouring when they received the trophy in a rain soaked ceremony on hallowed Wimbledon turf of the new number one court. This court had been covered with 730 metres of turf carefully removed from the All England Club's old number one court and transported to Eastbourne by lorry in an operation funded by the LTA, the borough

Monica Seles holds up the handsome Direct Line Championship trophy for the photographers.

The Legends Day players of 1996: (l to r) Owen Davison, Virginia Wade, Betty Stove, Ken Rosewall, Fred Stolle, Hana Mandlikova, Rosie Casals and Tony Roche.

council and Direct Line. With it came some items of Wimbledon memoribilia – a net and posts and some bench seating – to form the basis of a museum of tennis.

The Legends Day introduced on the first Monday of the Ladies Championships in 1996 was repeated in 1997 and proved so popular that the council entered into an agreement with Advantage International to present a series of Legends events throughout July and August featuring such players as Ilie Nastase, Peter Fleming, Vijay Armitraj and Roscoe Tanner.

11

EASTBOURNE – TOP TOWN
FOR TENNIS

One hundred and twenty five years ago a plot of land, 'eleven and a half acres in extent, situated to the west of the town and near Eastbourne College', was appropriated by the 7th Duke of Devonshire 'for the purposes of cricket and as a recreation ground'. When it opened to the public, without a ceremony of any kind, on July 1, 1874, it had a cricket pitch, terraces, tree lined walks and very little else.

Today it has a £4.5 million International Lawn Tennis Centre with permanent seating, lifts to all levels, and facilities to ensure the future of

grass court tennis in Eastbourne well into the next millenium. The centre is so extensive there is little room in the park for anything else – except, of course, for the Congress Theatre, the Congress Restaurant and patio restaurant, the Congress Village, the Devonshire Carvery and Buffet in the Winter Garden, the Devonshire Village with its Cavendish hospitality suite, and the Devonshire Park Theatre.

Buried in a time capsule beneath a new walkway in the centre are mementoes of people and events in the history of Eastbourne, chosen and assembled by pupils of Willingdon Trees Primary School. Not surprisingly most of their items of choice are from today rather than yesterday – a tennis ball signed by Tim Henman, a poster of Steffi Graf, and old and new maps and postcards of the resort. . . nothing to recall the rolling skating rink opened in 1875 with a display of skating by J L Plimpton, president of the New York Roller Skating Association, and his two daughters; the al fresco concerts in the Sycamore Grove; the bicycle races round the park perimeter; the croquet tournaments; the archery; the athletics meetings; the Indian Pavilion; the old Devonshire Baths and the badminton courts that went with them. . .

The past of the park has, however, been preserved in the Eastbourne Heritage Centre in Carlisle Road. It is open throughout the summer and well worth a visit. It is preserved too in the memories of those who have lived and worked here all their lives. Like 87 year old Molly Barton (nee Stevens) who lives just behind Devonshire Park and now regards it as her 'garden', although there was a time when she was unable to use the park at all:

'If you live where I do, where else do you go? You go up there. I am often the only person in the park, especially in the autumn and winter when there are not many people about.

I can remember as a little girl being taken there by my mother to watch various events, but it was very much a case of 'them and us'. If you bought a ticket you could go in but you were put behind a rope, well away from the members, and they didn't encourage just anyone to join as you might not be the right type of person.

I can't remember much about my father but I do know he must have belonged to it in some way because he used to go roller skating on the outdoor rink. My mother was born on December 29 1877, the night of the great storm when the pier was blown away, and I can remember a friend of hers telling me about a ball they had at the Floral Hall. It was called the Calico Ball and everyone had to wear cotton calico and my mother's friend, who seemed to me as old as the hills, got first prize for her dress. The manager when I was young was a Mr Mockett and he lived in what is now the Heritage Centre, which was the park manager's house. His daughter was the same age as my older sister and they went to the High School together. I know Mary used to go to one or two things with the Mockett girl as she could get in, being the manager's daughter.

There was never any chance of my going to play tennis there or anything because it was far too expensive, and although it was meant to be a park for the people of Eastbourne it never was, it was far too snooty.

When the council bought it that made all the difference because then it was opened up and people could use it. When it was privately owned ninety per cent of the people of Eastbourne couldn't use it, so we knew nothing about it and we couldn't care less about it. When the council asked us if they should purchase it of course we said, 'no way.'

It's entirely different now and I love it there. It is most interesting to watch the men mowing the grass tennis courts as they have to do it a certain way. I am told only one person knows how it is done and how it is looked after, and that is the Head Groundsman.**'**

David Lake, Events and Recreation manager from 1960 to 1991, remembers was taken as a child to the Children's Corner 'because that was the thing to do.'

'My first memory of the tennis side was when I was at the Grammar School and the geography master, a man called George Henshaw, had a summer job in Devonshire Park and he used to arrange for a squad of grammar school boys to go down and be ball boys for the South of England Championships.

No training was given. I hadn't even seen a tennis court up close until that time, so how we did it I don't know and I dread to think what the players thought of us. That went on most years and I remember going there twice and I think I received the princely sum of threepence after one day's ball-boying.

The outdoor skating rink had broken up long before my time, but there was still skating indoors at the Winter Garden. That finished in the mid to late fifties and there were two things that influenced the decision to end it. In roller skating you go on a whip – a crowd of you link arms and form a long line – and somebody came off the end of the whip going very fast and went into one of the pillars and was killed. That started people saying skating was dangerous, also the skates really damaged the surface and the council was faced with an enormous bill for replacing the dance floor.

I can just about remember the Indian Pavilion. It was one of the first things that came down when they built the Congress Theatre. I went across to the tennis office in 1960, although I had joined the council before that, and things were beginning to change. We worked in the old entrance to the park, formerly the ticket office and boardroom in the old Devonshire Park and Baths Company days.**'**

Janet Newton, who ran County Sports at Bexhill with her husband, Melvin, for twenty five years, sadly died of cancer last July. The shop has sold clothing and equipment at Devonshire Park for the past eighteen years and Janet, who was born, grew up and married at Eastbourne, was always in the firm's tent at the tournaments:

'I used to go roller skating in the Winter Garden which was fabulous, because of course there were no ice skating rinks anywhere near and it was something different. I also used to go to the Big Band concerts in the Fifties in the Winter Garden. They had people like Syd Lawrence and Joe Loss and it used to be an absolute sell out. We would stand in front of the stage, this was long before I met Melvin, and people would just be enthralled and there was never any trouble. We would have a good bop and a good listen.

As for the park itself, my father built the squash court – he was Llewellyn, the builder – and he also laid the floor in the Devonshire Park Theatre. He always boasted he laid that floor under the influence of eighteen gallons of lemonade because he was a staunch teetotaller in those days.

I played squash at Devonshire Park before I was married. Not many women played squash in the 1950s so I played with the boys from the rugby club. In fact it was Melvin who taught me to play the game. I was more interested in squash in those days than I was in tennis.'

Melvin took up the story:

'I was a Yorkshireman who moved to Eastbourne and I was a member of the Eastbourne Rugby Club. We would hire the Indian Pavilion for dances and I remember it looked very elaborate from the outside, but inside it was just one square room, rather like a church hall.

Janet and I used to play squash on the old courts, in the original building. In those days they were the only two squash courts in the area. I can remember Janet's uncle, Eric Llewellyn, telling me the squash courts were of a special American design and it was one of the first buildings built like that.

At the end of the war you could buy a pair of Green Flash tennis shoes for a guinea and a squash ball for nine old pence, which is less than 5p. A squash racket again was about a guinea and the old professional there always had rackets to sell.

Although they had quite good showers we always went across to Devonshire Baths for a swim after we had played. At one time the Rugby Club used to change in the Devonshire Baths and they had these huge slipper baths where the controls were outside for either hot or cold ordinary water or hot or cold sea water. The trick was to wait until you had your bath and then go outside and alter the control to pour a bit of cold sea water in and it was always rusty.'

Visitor Maurice Brown supports his home county of Northampton but each year, during the LTA Inter County Grass Court Championships, he transfers his support to the counties in Group One at Eastbourne.

'I would love to support Northampton, but they play at some rather strange venues. I like Eastbourne and have been coming down for about fifteen years for County Week. I used to come to the Junior Tennis as well until unfortunately Eastbourne lost that.

The most important thing for me is the tennis is played on grass in Devonshire Park. To me, tennis is grass. When you watch it in France it's fine, but you've got brick dust blowing everywhere from the courts and it's always so hot and dusty.

One of the best matches I've ever seen played in Eastbourne was when sixteen year old Sam Smith met Clare Wood, who was seeded Number One, in the Eighteen and Under Nationals. She lost the first set and the second set reached a tie break with Sam 0-6 down. Then she won eight straight points in a row to take the set and went on to take the match. It was an absolute marathon, an incredible match.

There have been some wonderful matches here and, particularly in County Week, some sad ones. One year two counties were battling it out for fourth or fifth place. To stay in fourth place one particular county had to win just one matchout of the last three. Two were lost very quickly, but the middle game went on and on and everyone was standing there waiting for the girls to win and they lost. One of the girls was inconsolable and they couldn't get her off the court because she felt it was all her fault. The fact that everybody else had lost was no consolation to her and that just about sums up County Week for me. There is a terrific atmosphere and emotions run very high.'

Stan Patch, a steward at the championships from 1987 until he retired in 1995, was not at all sure about the new stadium when it first opened.

'It's a lovely stand and it's very modern but I think we have lost the feeling of intimacy we used to have when we were in our nice little wooden boxes.

We built up a good rapport with our regular customers over the years and some of my dear ladies have told me they find the concrete just a bit too hard, they would rather have the old wood seats. I know it burnt down and obviously was a fire hazard, but there was such a feeling of 'we belong here'. In the new stand some of the people who have been coming for years and years say they feel they are now 'just a number now' but it's progress and I suppose we'll get used to it. One of my clearest memories of the old stands is of the birds nesting in the roof and it's rather sad all that has gone.'

Players, too, have affectionate memories of Eastbourne, and they, obviously, have the most informed views about the new centre. Former British Number One Jo Durie, told *Eastbourne Herald* reporter, Amanda Wilkins, that she misses her competitive days at Devonshire Park:

'This is where I played my first match at the age of eleven and I came here every single year after that until I retired.

I still come down to watch the Ladies Championships and to run coaching sessions with Alan Jones, but it is not quite the same.

I always loved playing at Eastbourne. I knew that the next week at Wimbledon would be terribly tiring but in Devonshire Park I could walk around and practice when I wanted to. I have usually had my family with me and we would make a holiday of it.

I've seen all the changes over the years and, although it was a bit of a shock to walk in and see a great big concrete structure instead of the old stands, I think they've done it very nicely and the centre court is lovely to play on. All the players like it.'

Martina Navratilova, who between 1982 and 1993 virtually made the Eastbourne Ladies International Championships her own tournament, winning the singles eleven times and the doubles six times, told Amanda:

‘When I arrived at Devonshire Park for the tournament I felt I'd come to the wrong place. I thought I was in Birmingham.

I turned the corner and the first thing that went through my mind was 'Oh God, I didn't think the place would be so different'. But once I had got used to it I don't think the centre has lost anything, it's just a different setting, but it makes a better court, there's no question about that.

When I played here before the old North Stand burnt down, I noticed that there was always the same two elderly ladies sitting in the same seats at the front each year. It became a ritual for me, after the final match, to go over and hand them my bouquet.

Eastbourne now is a great play-

Martina at one of her last press conferences.

ing stadium because most of it is there all the time, whereas when we play on the outdoor facilities elsewhere in the world most of them are temporary. They just erect the stands for a week and take them down again.

It's always nice to play in a place that is permanent and it is definitely a change for the better. I loved the Eastbourne tournament anyway and would always look forward to coming back again the next year.’

Jana Novotna and Arantxa Sanchez Vicario shared the singles title in 1997.

12

CHAMPION WOMEN

EASTBOURNE'S pre-Wimbledon tennis championships are today worth a massive £3 million to the town each year in advertising and extra business. Director of Tourism Ronald Cussons splits this up into £1 million towards the general economy of the resort from vastly increased business for hotels and restaurants, shops and places of entertainment.

Championships director George Hendon agrees. 'At the end of each championship, even before had the new centre, people have immediately booked seats for the following year – and booked their hotel accommodation a year in advance as well,' he said.

With such headlined players as there were in the 1998 draw – seven times Wimbledon champion Steffi Graf, Aranta Sanchez Vicario, Jana Novotna and rising young stars like Moscow-born teenager Anna

MORE PAST WINNERS

Lori McNeil (USA), (pictured above) won the 1992 singles title. Above right is Meredith McGrath (USA), unseeded winner in 1994 and (right) Nathalie Tauziat (France), 1995 singles winner.

Jana Novotna, last year's Eastbourne and Wimbledon singles champion, will be back here in June to defend her title.

Kournikova and 6ft 2ins tall Venus Williams with her beaded dreadlocks and her sister, Serena – the coverage by the national and international media was worth at least £2 million to the town.

'That is money we could not possibly afford to spend on publicity,' said Ron Cussons. 'The whole thing is quite fantastic . . .'

THE EASTBOURNE CHAMPIONS
YEAR BY YEAR

1975 Virginia Wade bt Billie Jean King 7-5, 4-6, 6-4
*1976 Chris Evert bt Virginia Wade 8-6, 6-3.
1977 Federation Cup USA bt Australia.
*1978 Martina Navratilova bt Chris Evert 6-4, 4-6, 9-7.
*1979 Chris Evert-Lloyd bt Martina Navratilova 7-5, 5-7, 13-11
1980 Tracey Austin bt Wendy Turnbull 7-6, 6-2
1981 Tracey Austin bt Andrea Jaeger 6-3, 6-4
*1982 Martina Navratilova bt Hana Mandlikova 6-4, 6-3
1983 Martina Navratilova bt Wendy Turnbull 6-1, 6-1
1984 Martina Navratilova bt Kathy Jordan 6-4, 6-2
1985 Martina Navratilova bt Helena Sukova 6-4, 6-3
1986 Martina Navratilova bt Helena Sukova 3-6, 6-3, 6-4
1987 Helena Sukova bt Martina Navratilova 7-6, 6-3
1988 Martina Navratilova bt Natalia Zvereva 6-2, 6-2
1989 Martina Navratilova bt Raffaela Reggi 7-6, 6-2
*1990 Martina Navratilova bt Gretchen Magers 6-0, 6-2
1991 Martina Navratilova bt Arantxa Sanchez Vicario 6-4, 6-4
1992 Lori McNeil bt Linda Harvey-Wild 6-4, 6-4.
1993 Martina Navratilova bt Miriam Oremans 2-6, 6-2, 6-3
1994 Meredith McGrath bt Linda Harvey-Wild 6-2, 6-4
1995 Natalie Tauziat bt Chanda Rubin 3-6, 6-0, 7-5
1996 Monica Seles bt Mary Jo Fernandez 6-0, 6-2.
1997 Jana Novotna and Arantxa Sanchez Vicario. Rain stopped final.
*1998 Jana Novotna bt Arantxa Sanchez Vicario 6-1, 7-5.
1999

A star * indicates a same-year singles win at Wimbledon.

INDEX

INDEX

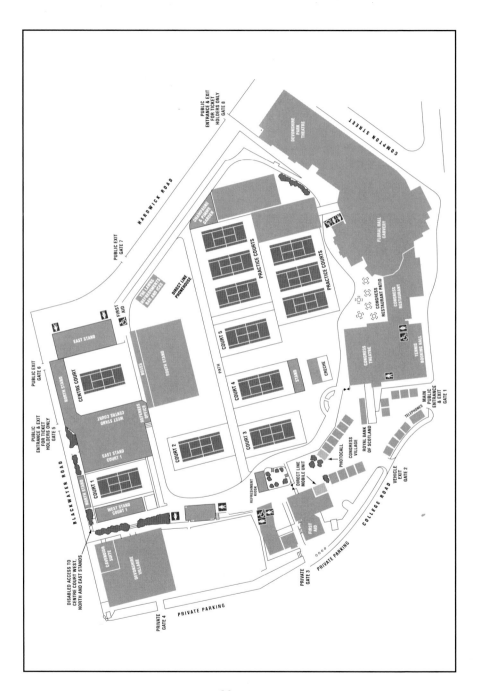